Broken Soul

by
Victor Comori I

kingpencomori@gmail.com

ISBN: 978-1-7346976-0-5

Published by Jadacovers

bit-urls.com/98054

Contents

Acknowledgements

This is a very special project for me. Broken Soul was originally written between the years 1998-2004. Finally, in the year 2020 this book is in worldwide publication. I never woke up and said that I wanted to be a writer. All I know is that I always woke up and wrote. I always had a creative spirit and realized I'm most happy when I'm creating. I thought I had an interesting take on life and wanted to share my view point. I never wanted to be famous I just always loved music which led to my love for words and writing lyrics. I wrote my first rap at 11 years old from that point on I've been hooked on words. I preach literacy, yes reading and writing. My mother taught me early in life how to read and write. These two skills helped me significantly in my life. Now as I move forth in life, I've decided to take my passion to write into a writing career which encompasses books, music, movies and tv scripts. My mom passed away in 2010, but she inspired me and continues to inspire me. So, today I'm letting my mother Deborah Ann Jackson know you were right I have become more than what the streets offered. Self expression, has become my salvation and I thank God for that. I don't know what kind of writer my peers may describe me as. What I do know is that my passion is this pen and I'm at my best when I'm scribbling thoughts. These thoughts became songs, these songs became books and these books will become movies and for me that is infinite joy. So today I dedicate this book to my mother Deborah Ann Jackson, my grandmother Eleanora Honey Jackson, my grandmother Annie McCord and my aunt Rosa Elaine Davis. I thank you all for what you have contributed to the man that I have become today.

Foreword

Broken Soul is a poetry book with a social, political and community point of view, all from the mind of a physically incarcerated man. The reflective thoughts of Victor Comori are on an array of subjects ranging from his love for his mother to his indifferences with the justice system. The poems were written between the year 1998-2004. Classic soul gripping poetry from a man in search of redemption witness his broken soul.

iv

Rap Star

How can I aid the struggle?

When my own people in a huddle

Conspiring to stop me,

Like I'm the motherfuckin enemy!

All I wanna do is, stop the cycle.

Reproduce a new breed of Africans.

Get into the mind of the masses

Then give them divine vision

Through their Cartier glasses

Now I no longer entertain the bullshit

I've been in prison for damn near 10

Put away the childish things today

We are now boys to men

Who and why do they congregate on Capitol Hill?

Who is it responsible for our incarceration?

Locked behind steel

Then why y'all fuckin with me?

Oh yea, rap means something when the message is real.

It's all good when I talk about drugs and gat's

Smoking blunts and chasin hoes, when dey asses fat

But when I preach about the beast, that keep us niggas in
chains

Y'all tell me keep the peace, money in the rap game.

Now we high and we fly

Get any thang money can buy

Can't even look yo momma in the eye

Yo mama know you're living a lie.

Platinum records can't help us

Overcome these times

We keep dancing and smoking

We got diamonds that shine

Being wealthy aint always healthy

Especially when your spirit is poor

You always crave for more

More drugs, more alcohol, more sex, more money

More name brand clothes

So we can look more stunnin

And if I have to carry it like this

I pray my music career miss

I can't see myself living like this

I wanna be more than just a rap star...rap star

Prison Eyez

Look here youngsta, What's on your mind man?

Give me a little bit of your time man

Watch dem suckas that you run with

They might drop a dime man

Oh, you trust dem?

Because you gang bang with dem

And you slang 'caine with dem?

Oh to you I'm just another nigga scared straight

And just because I no longer sell dope

You think I'm dead weight?

If you look into my eyez

You'll see the guns, the dope, the Fed time

I was bad (dumb) in my prime

Young nigga I made the headlines

look into my heart and tell me what you see?

A boy transformed into a man

And yes I disagree

With you throwing your life away

The hood is twisted like the cap on a Hen bottle

My eyez get misty

Because I know you won't stop until the pen holler

Respect your existence

Nothing from nothing leaves nothing

But you are flesh and blood

Please let mama rest

She loves, she loves

What God allowed her to create

Even if it was with a scandalous mate

She always made sure you ate

Even if she had to take a date

Surrender while still ignorant

This way you give yourself a chance to be wise

I'm telling you this in hindsight

My point of view through prison eyez.

Destiny

How many people really live their destiny?

How many of us, are really on the path the God's intended?

How do you know if your significant other is your soul mate?

I ask these questions in search of an invisible purpose

Sometimes life is like having no light in a dark room

You feel your way to the door

But once you make it to the door, what's next?

If only I could confront the impossible dream

Then manifest it for all the true believers

Give them a glimpse at what the future holds,

And foil all attempts by their deceivers

Why not achieve?

Don't you believe?

Doesn't your mind conceive images and thoughts of glory?

Sometimes we must become iconoclastic

To avoid the pitfalls of life

Control your own vision

Then tell your own story

Who are you?

Why are you here?

Clarify these questions your real purpose is near

Are you the rose or the thorn?

Don't you wanna know why you were born?

For only one reason

Even though different seasons

Your destiny doesn't change

No matter what you do to your physical attributes

or your name

Your destiny is the same

What you become, is what you claim

Love Or Hate

You're no friend of mine.

You can't be any kin of mine.

When I'm down you kick.

When I'm on top you love Vic.

I'll rather you eradicate yourself from my space.

Let me breathe alone.

Let me die alone.

Our whole vibe is wrong.

This is now a rival zone.

Conflict, confusion, betrayal

I know you're not to be trusted.

You pray to see me suffer.

It brings you joy when I'm disgusted.

I'm the dog, you're the cat.

You're the cat, I'm the rat.

You're the rat, I'm the snake.

Where there's no love

There must be hate.

I'm Iraq, you're the U.S

One to the head, two to da chest.

Do I think you would murder me?

Yes!

At times the truth does kill!

Four letter word love.

Four letter word hate.

Which master is better to serve?

Stuck in the crossroads

We don't know whether to smile or explode.

I initiate peace

But war is never too far from my mind.

My lower self is the beast.

My higher self I've yet to find.

I've maintained my position as a man

And I stand like a God.

But my life is still not leveled

As I contemplate thoughts of the devil.

Final decision, as I decide with precision

Which road should I take?

Still stuck in the crossroads.

Will it be love?

Or

Will it be hate?

Mixed Emotions

\What have you contributed to my life as a father?

What part of my character did you help build?

You gave me nothing, but am I nothing?

They say I must be something because I live.

Part of me hates you for not being there,

Part of me love you for the time we did share.

I don't remember you chastising me.

I don't remember you hugging me,

Tell me did you even care?

All you left me was an absent touch.

A absent look

A absent mind to explore

Now my present life,

At this present time,

I resent your presence.

Though you're not absent anymore,

My world is divided with you.

This is one with mixed emotions.

But yet, I've confided in you.

I'm still one with mixed emotions.

I see your courage and I smile.

That's the same courage that I have.

I see your heart and it's like mine too.

That smile turns into a laugh.

You're very head strong and competitive,

And you always speak your mind.

I'm competitive and head strong too,

And I say what I feel all the time.

I thought you had left me with nothing,

But you gave me something after all.

Now I realize without you,

I would not exist.

You made me something after all

And though we hardly ever agree,

I see a medium approaching.

On this we both agree,

We love each other with mixed emotions.

Insignificant Breath

Shall I die for you all.

Shall I give you my food and water.

Since my life is not my own,

Perhaps I should fulfill that order.

When you live for the people,

you take insignificant breaths.

Yet every breath is significant

when you're breathing for everyone else.

If I could only be sacrificed,

While simultaneously edifying my clan

My death will be serene.

Here lies one happy man.

You without I shall prosper,

I without you shall fail.

If I can't unite my people,

How can I lead them out this hell?

Liberty flows through my veins,

My heart pounds justice

Equality fuels my mind

Yet slavery still exist.

I been failed by the justice system,

And the way we are treated,

Really hasn't changed over time.

Then why do I still feel committed to change?

Is a question I constantly ask.

You can't eradicate what's in the heart and soul of a man

No matter what.

He works diligently to accomplish his task.

I'm driven eternally,

It's always me for you.

Me for you, me for you.

Self-importance dies with the struggle,

Now flesh can't control what I say or do.

Will I be labeled a militant thinker,

Or will they honor the truth with respect

People label those they fear.

Praying to god the truth,

We all will reject.

Shall I die for you all.

Shall I give you my food and water.

Since my life is not my own,

Perhaps I should fulfill that order.

When you live for the people,

you take insignificant breaths.

Yet every breath is significant

when you're breathing for everyone else.

Mind Freeworld

You live in the Freeworld

I live in the mind Freeworld.

You have no physical restraints,

But mentally you're impeded.

I have no mental restraints

But physically I'm impeded

Now you tell me who's really free?

Thoughts of who I am,

What can I be?

What can I create?

Invade my daydreams

(Mind Freeworld)

They tell you who you are

What you can be

And that they will create all you need (Freeworld)

The sky is the limit

Nothing is impossible

An idea is the first sign of a genius (Mind Freeworld)

Your life is limited

Nothing is possible

An idea is just an idle thought in your head (Freeworld)

You make your own decisions

You control your own visions

You're making positive progression day by day (Mind Freeworld)

Someone is thinking of you

Someone is directing your aspirations

Now your conditions impede your progress (Freeworld)

I'm in a mind Freeworld

You live In the Freeworld

My mind is free in my world

Your mind is enslaved in your world.

Now you tell me who's really free?

What Is Loss?

The world is at loss.

Our youth are faced with guns.

The things we lose in the rain

We just may find in the sun.

If my son dies

And your son lives

But goes to prison with a life sentence

With whom do we place our empathy?

Two different scenarios

Two identical emotions

Somebody please explain loss to me.

A child grows to be a young man or a young lady

Somewhere along the way

A mother feels as if she's lost a baby.

Physically here

But no longer close enough

To reduce that fear.

Maybe my multifacet view point on the word loss.

Will spare me pain many years from now.

My conscious ignorance helps me focus

On what I've obtained, from what I've lost.

Now through what I've lost some how I have gained.

Years in prison has balanced out to

Wisdom, patience and discipline.

May the scales of life be tipped in my favor.

May the hell in life miss me and my neighbor.

The testimony of the innocent

Shall stand the test of time.

Through all her days she'll never meet defeat

Though she mingles with the guilty.

She's identified by her shine.

But what if she lost that shine?

Does it take away from all she's gained?

Is she any less innocent?

Is there any more pain?

We all pay for life

But what exactly is the cost?

Focus on what you can gain.

Even in the mist of what you've lost.

Family Destroyed (HIV)

How come he got H.I.V?

How come he got H.I.V?

How come I don't have H.I.V?

She was such a beautiful woman.

He was such a handsome man.

I look ok myself

I'm glad that condom was close at hand.

She lived right next door to me

Very attractive, very fine.

He played football at my high school

The dude was way before his time.

I knew them both, but I still can't believe

They both got H.I.V.

Did she give it to him?

Or did he give it to her?

More importantly who's going to raise their daughter?

They're both looking bad and getting worse.

Man, I hate to see her suffer!

Man, I hate to see his pain!

Word on the street.

She was cheating down the block

With ole what's his name.

Y'all know the rumors.

They're just like tumors.

They just grow and grow.

The fact is that they both got H.I.V.

Who gave it to who, we will never know.

Partial Recollection

Today I'm to a point where I know what I know.

Spiritually and mentally, I know I must grow.

No one has awakened the dormant potential in me.

I realize I'm not utilizing something meant just for me.

My purpose starts to surface as I nurture my spirit.

I've been searching for resolve now I feel it and hear it.

What man shall see his destiny emerge before face.

If he doesn't know himself, his history or his place.

Consider me what I am, what I am is what you see.

Divine, sometimes falsely defined, denied by me.

I reconcile with my soul, we're both feeling betrayed.

By the physical realm of our existence everything man made.

Have you ever been to the point where you just know what

you know?

No written instructions or directions you just go where you go.

Then once you get there you feel the power from the course you've traveled.

Then every mystery in your life somehow becomes unraveled.

How did I get here? I don't know. I just know what I know.

And when you get there, you won't know, you'll just know what you know.

Still Going Under

I guess you don't have anything to fear.

When your misinformed and miseducated

About the ways of the world.

Lord knows we need help.

The green earth he created has been invaded.

By creatures who do everything the opposite of his nature.

Man it doesn't take much, for man to hate ya.

Ladies it doesn't take smut for man to rape ya.

SICK minds!

Somehow find serenity in the decimation of others.

Look at what dem red neck suckers did to James Byrd.

And we wonder why the youth in the hood smoke herb.

Maybe they are tired of burying their peers.

Maybe their tired of the state and federal years.

I could care less if the whole world went up in smoke.

What I see is not what I live for.

But after all I am looking through prison eyes.

My mind holds steadfast to this conviction.

That I can somehow, some way change the world

Through my spoken word.

After all God said let it be and it was.

But society says that I'm not God.

Or am I God? Didn't God come in the image of man?

If so someone on earth has to have the power make a difference.

Now that's something to think about.

As we keep going under.

Just a lil something to ponder.

While we're still going under.

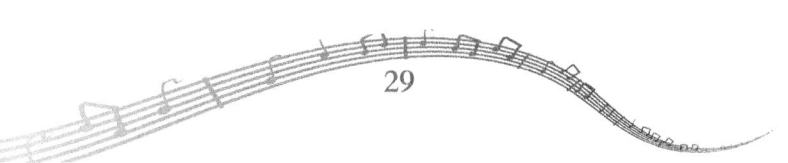

29

Grandma Annie

I never felt as if she had what she deserved

While here on earth.

In her new home I pray she's given

All she's worth.

How can the family ever be the same?

My grandma left me as fast as she came

I remember her smooth brown skin.

I remember a face that couldn't sin.

I remember her teaching us how to be men.

I just want to see my grandma again.

While I was in prison she just slipped away.

March 7th, I cried and cried that day.

All I could do was smoke a J.

Hoping the pain somehow went away.

She said she would be there when I got home.

She said she would be there when I got home.

But she a'int there, we can't talk on the phone.

Man life ain't fair.

Why my grandma ain't home?

I made her so many promises in the visiting room.

When she left me, she said she would be back to visit me soon

I never seen her again, God took her to soon.

I never seen her again, God took her to soon.

And I still love my grandma Annie.

And I'll never stop loving my grandma Annie.

I give my eternal love to my grandma Annie.

Where ever you are I love you grandma Annie.

Gangsta

What made you?

Was it the power that they gave you?

Influencing young minds with the propaganda of a gangsta.

Consciously traveling down the wrong road.

But this time you have an innocent passenger in back.

Why want you save one!

Why not free one soul tonight?

Let that boy know it's ok to be black.

Teach him different ways to survive and make dat paper stack!

Sacrifice yourself!

Don't let that youngsta life go down the drain!

Don't make him feel your pain!

Look at that innocent smile.

Don't mislead that innocent child!

I'm talkin to you gangsta!

Change is now home boi!

Don't blame shit for the thangs you destroy!

I'm offering you a chance to be a real man.

School that youngsta give him a different plan.

One that will stop him from killin his brother!

One that will stop him from disrespectin his mother!

Believe it or not you can do that gangsta.

That boy look up to you.

You are his O.G.

You are what he one day aspires to be.

Save that child now!

Tomorrow may be too late!

It will break my heart to visit his wake

I'm asking you this one favor.

Give that boy something positive to change his behavior.

Stanley Williams even reached out from the pen.

That's just what we do, when we are face to face with our sins.

Now here's your chance for Redemption.

Make the most of it and save that child.

Who walks like you!

Who talks like you!

Because he to one day wants to be a

GANGSTA!

Behind Bars

Behind bars all I see is African faces.

Men far removed from African places.

Charged with murder, robbery and drugs.

Does a bias system exist?

Yes It does!

I wander how many of these white boys

Gon end up with state or federal time?

Yes I am pulling the race card!

I need, we need the race card!

The young, black male should be crying!

Every time one of da homeboys enters the court room

for sentencing, we eagerly await.

You read the time on his face when he returns.

5-10. Whew he's just glad it's over.

15-20 years he wears a crooked smile.

25-30 years he understands he has just entered

a stage called stripped liberty.

30 or more he's internally destroyed.

His head held low as we try our best to console him.

Even though our own lives are still in jeopardy.

Behind bars weak men fiend for other men.

A mental sickness in a freak environment.

Behind bars a strong man dreams of a blissful marriage with
kids.

Meticulous plans for his retirement.

The contrast and parity are part of both worlds.

Both worlds referring to your free world and my mind free
world.

The nature of man will always remain the same.

Self- preservation is rule number one.

That will never change.

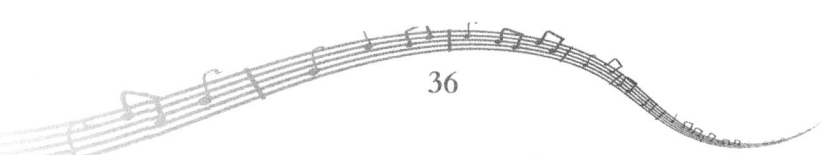

I'm behind bars, you're behind bars.

We're all behind bars to a certain extent.

The real Victor is the man

Who has the desire to break the bars

Through his will he circumvents.

As I Travel

Today I feel as if I'm slippin.

Or perhaps I've already slipped.

When a nigga like me should be grippin.

It' feels as if I'm losing my grip.

I'm mesmerized by the vistas.

That flash through my mind.

Who saw em coming with dem burners.

While I'm lost on the grind.

Everlasting life , I hold that promise to God.

How can I ever love a wife with a heart that's been scarred.

Some people see me as a genius with unlimited talent.

But even as a genius my life seems off balance.

I hold on to dear life and I cherish each breath.

I'll impact the world twice.

With my birth and my death.

Though I contradict my convictions

My vision is divine.

God says complete the mission.

If you seek you shall find.

Come My Queen

My spiritual journey turns left, then turns right.

My heart is yearning for peace but I fight and I fight.

My discipline wavers locked down, who can save us?

Prison is not the answer.

I advance my pawns sacrificing them in my quest for a queen.

Me being a king has no perks.

My life is still unfulfilled in my dreams.

Who loves a man away?

Who loves a man that sometimes doesn't pray?

Many questions, few answers

Complicated yet facile.

And yes I did pray before my evening meal.

I was raised to be a serene man but somehow my bestial
thoughts

Extirpated the serenity from my heart.

Now I'm miles apart from what I should be.

But a sacrifice away from what I could be.

If you hear me help me.

If you're near me accept me

Aint no love lost my grudge soft.

Come to me my Queen. Come to me my Queen.

Perfect Love

What a beautiful smile she has.

So young and innocent as she glides past.

I thank God for the female.

They're the reason why we are well.

I wander if she'll be appreciated.

When she's older enough to understand what appreciation really is.

I pray she's not emotionally scarred

Or physically abused.

I hope she one day connects with a man

That stimulates her mind and understand

She's not to be misused.

Go on and grow my little angel.

I pray we raise sons

Who will instantly recognize your worth.

Someone who will protect you from danger.

Someone who understands you're the water of this earth.

It's essential that you connect with someone

Who helps unveil your potential.

Someone to help solve your problems.

In the mist of your confusion.

Your knight in shining armor

But not one from a book.

That's an illusion.

P.R.E.C.I.O.U.S

Oh yes!

I realize we're blessed

A woman. The love an intuition side of a man.

Draw near take my hand.

Let's expand our horizons together.

Let's fascinate the world with our love.

Isn't that what you want baby girl?

Isn't that much better than a hug?

I appreciate your beauty.

But what I really admire is your mind.

I want to spend time in your head.

The perfect place to wine and dine.

Now does that sound romantic?

If so please don't panic.

Just relax and love shall appear.

Just ask his highness will make it clear

But for now I'll disappear like a ghost.

Choose the man who loves you the most.

Even then you won't experience the perfect love.

Stand By Me

I'm incarcerated man.

I don't understand.

No one will stand by me.

A man should stand.

I guess they can't stand me.

I don't understand.

I know I left in a hurry.

I never said goodbye.

When I left she left.

She never said goodbye.

It's hard in here.

But some how I'm getting by.

I've attained much wisdom.

That money couldn't buy.

Nobody's loving me.

So I'm loving myself.

If It wasn't for me

I'll be by myself.

Now It's all about me.

I see no one else.

If yall can't stand by me.

I'll stand by myself!

Survive The Fire

All I want to do is get out the fire.

Raise my kids, have some of the things I desire.

Once again I find myself in the mist of the furnace.

Tap dancing on everything I've learned.

Praying I make it through, trying not to get burned.

Dealing with people I really don't trust.

Appease them with payment.

Making them think it's about us.

I see and smell the smoke.

But the last promise I made to myself I've already broke.

My path to victory is paved.

If I make it through history is made.

Is it worth the gamble?

Or should I gather my things up and scramble?

If I play it cool things should go smooth.
So I B Quiet, B Patient, and B Thinking.
They think I'm paranoid.
But only if they knew the success I'm after
And the trouble I'm trying to avoid.

I'm in the fire again.
I can't do another day in the pen.
I keep my enemies close
and watch my friends.

Is this a sane way to live?
Considering my aspirations, I think it is.
Constantly walking on coals.
I've tried like hell to turn my flames of desire
into a smolder.

But it burns, it burns so bad.

I want success but sometimes the price is expensive.

As I move with grace.

There's no stress on my face.

But all the while I'm just trying to survive the fire.

Don't Self Destruct

Wandering the streets day and night

He picked up quickly.

Survival depends on his willingness to fight.

Sleeping pillar to post.

In search of one good meal.

And for that he will steal.

Though he has no desire to kill.

If he will steal he has the capacity to kill.

He is the product of his environment.

His mother nor father never saw retirement

But they both retired.

One from a drug overdose.

The other from gunfire.

He's old enough to have a job and be hired.

But before the interview he's already fired.

Victim of stereotypes.

You know the gold teeth, dreadlocked hair thang?

He has little understanding.

Walking around with a false name.

\

So much potential locked inside

But he has no key.

No route to victory.

Remember his family history is marred with mockery.

Prison, poverty and death

Creeped up on all his role models.

He lost the woman that loved him most.

Now he's stuck in an ol liquor bottle.

Down on his luck.

Stuck on his butt.

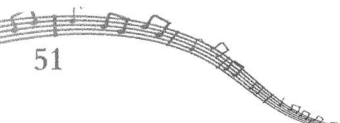

A volcano that's about to erupt.

Now he's become the perfect example of what it means to

Self destruct.

Sunday Dinner

If only you'll stay alive to see me rise

Above what you've previously seen.

Far beyond your wildest dreams.

Every night I ask God

To keep the blood pumping in your heart.

And to make your body healthy.

Strong enough to live to witness me wealthy.

Not just monetarily but spiritually.

I know your pillow is still wet with tears

From the way a child you gave birth to just up and disappeared.

But I'm here mama

And you're still so dear mama

And please express my love to grandma honey.

Tell her I'm doing well

And faith will keep her alive.

Her only wish is to see my brother and I

Come home before she dies.

This seems like a race against time.

A desperate attempt to reach out and touch

Two women that I love.

Without the wandering eyes of these confines.

Am I sorry for my transgressions?

I don't think so. No, not sorry.

Sorry is such a poor word.

I feel more like a redeemer.

As if I should give them something remarkable.

Equal to the pain and tears of ten years away.

But all I really want is one more Sunday dinner

With my mother and grandmother.

Simply to express our true feelings.

And to show just how much the love is reciprocated.

But if they're taken away from me before I arrive

There's no death when the spirit is still alive.

I will still thank God for the time he granted.

Never question why.

Just understand it.

I'll move on and stay strong.

Though the road will be arduous and long.

I know my mother and my grandmother

Will always be there for Sunday dinner.

I'll never dine alone.

My Mothers Day

My mama, my drama, my life, my love.

My tears, my smiles, my heart, my hugs.

Aint nothing in this world that I want do for you.

The only woman in my life who was always true.

Through thick and thin.

When I was sick in the pen.

Through all my sins.

You were my mother and friend.

You never left me.

You kept me close to your heart

For 3,000 nights straight

A Federal sentence kept us apart.

My time away matured me into a man

Who can now appreciate the gift you gave to me.

The gift of life.

How you desire to see me with a wife.

I understand now mama.

I'm getting my life in order.

I'm raisings my sons and daughters.

I wanna be better for you.

As you wanna be better for me.

The mutual love and respect has grown.

You'll feel me deeper when I'm free.

You gave birth to me at age fifteen.

A child raising a child.

We were more like brother and sister.

So you understood me when I was wild.

Thank you, for you.

The pain and the joy.

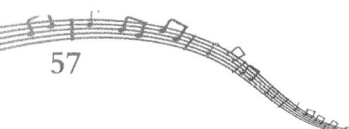

Through the drug addiction, the near evictions.

I'm still your baby boy.

Nothing can ever replace your smile and compassion.

Others may see faults in you.

But in my eyes you are the perfect woman.

Happiness is yours in abundance.

If you want it just show it.

If it cost a million dollars, I'll blow it.

You deserve everything from heaven to earth.

Even though with you, material things never mattered.

I can't even write or articulate.

The love I have for you.

But as you read this, I pray your heart beats

The way it beats when you know the love is true.

The roses and cards are great.

And I apologize sincerely for being away.

I love you infinitely year round.

And I wish you a Happy Mothers Day!

Spoken Word

Can't you peek the signs?

America is controlled by an elite few.

I'll keep you brothers posted.

I'm still investigating who.

But I know damn well lit can't be me.

Because if it were you brothers would be free.

Listen to me.

One night I awoke.

The spirit said get up and go help your folk.

And I said how?

Then she said what did God do?

I said he spoke.

Yes, with wisdom and love.

Yes, for the same people they now call thugs.

Yes, we can go back to what it was.

Are you familiar with Sankofa?

A beautiful African word.

S-A-N-K-O-F-A look it up.

No time to expound today.

I'm in the mist of observing the spoken word.

I give to you what has been so graciously bestowed upon me.

One brother told me

You may be the messenger or the prophet.

Because you speak the language of the people.

He said you know each movement has a sequel?

But can you lead the people?

I told him all I can give the people is my word.

My unwavering word.

Which I treat with royalty.

Which I express with loyalty.

Attentive ears listen they don't just hear.

The spoken word shall be here.

Long after we all disappear.

Don't follow trends.

Don't follow the ways of men.

Who deceive on the podium

Because they are versed in what they read.

Quoting scripture after scripture.

Consult your spirit before you believe.

But embrace the truth as if it were your mother.

Truth is similar to your mother.

Because it has the power to create a reflection of its self.

Multiple times over a child is born.

The truth is told.

A child is born the truth is told.

So stop searching for the truth.

You are the truth.

Now I conclude this is my spoken word.

Inspiration

Inspiration, inspiration.

Inspire an entire nation.

That's my desire.

The sole purpose which fuels my fire.

I pray I'm blessed by something higher.

Which means when I reach deep within

I come out with something greater each and every time.

I'm here to encourage, never discourage.

And you notice in each of those words

The key word is courage.

Find me arriving timely to speak to those in need.

As I proceed to curve my selfishness and greed.

I know it seems as if I'm moving at warp speed.

But it took a life time to renew my mind

To realign my peace of mind.

Though the world is still unkind

I stand here dressed in black.

Though my heart is no longer black

But my soul is.

Dark to the core.

Witness my African heart pour.

I'm raw man!

I've been face to face with the law man!

I'm giving you all that I saw man

In my world.

My broken soul.

I wanna help the ladies raise the babies.

I'm tired of being M.I.A.

and I don't mean that I was in Miami.

I was enslaved voluntarily.

Being held captive by my own mental capacity.

Now aint that something?

Being the slave and the slave master.

No wonder we continue to meet with disaster.

Now my eyes are open.

I'm doing much more than hoping.

I'm giving before I take.

I'm living not calling upon my wake.

And I do it because I wanna be an inspiration, inspiration.

A man who inspires an entire nation.

Time And Mind

Seconds, minutes, hours

Time is your power.

What you do with your time reveals to mankind

What's exactly on your mind.

There is no time to hate on another man's dream.

There is no time to get caught up in plots and schemes.

There is no time to get lost in the world of bling bling.

Use your time.

Use your mind.

Never walk through your day

Without taking a moment to pray.

No, everything is not ok.

Three minutes from now your whole world could be wiped

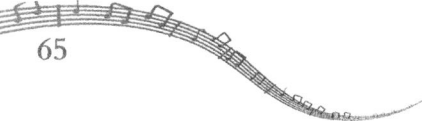

away.

I've seen tragedy catch up with men
Who should be addressed as your majesty.
But the king died before his time.
Or was it just his time?

Leave me for an hour and I promise to return to you
With wisdom through meditation.
Thoughts far from superficial.
My life is to real to be artificial.
I give to you the best part of me, my spirit.
The vision to see it embrace it an hear it, my spirit.
I had to do time to really understand time.
And now I truly know the value of mine.
Use your time.
Use your mind.

Desire

There is nothing in this world that can measure the reach of desire.

The height of high rises nor the skies can compare.

The man with the most talent sometimes may meet defeat.

The man with the most desire refuses to lose.

When I'm sad through my blues.

I strap on my shoes.

Then walk like a giant who rules this land.

After years in this cell I must understand

How I won. How I failed.

How to stay on my trail.

Not distracted or interacted with those who fell weak in times of duress.

I stay strong through hard times.

I'm what God designed

The signs tell me the nation is mine.

I never label it hard work.

I just work hard.

In the rain, snow, light and the dark.

So stubborn inside, never budge like a tank.

Take my position in stride then rise through the ranks.

Call me chief!

Put a desire to win on my wreath!

Non believers I make them just stare in disbelief.

I'm desire! I'm eternal!

I won't die! I can't bleed!

I now realize God equipped me with all that I need.

Dedication plants the seed for spiritual elevation.

Spiritual elevation gives birth to physical manifestation

Of all your subconscious thoughts.

But without desire all is lost.

No seeds to plant.

No dreams to grasp.

Images Of Strength

I salute those who did more than just talk.

The ones who were willing to sit in and or walk.

The ones that thought segregation was wrong.

He marched his kids to the so called "white school."

With equality on his mind.

All at the same time, Injustice is his reality.

His skin color is his crime.

Marked for life.

He's faithful to his kids and wife.

He sets an example that his seeds heed.

He's the real reason why they succeed.

I salute mothers who smile and cried

When the love came in disguise and lied.

The ones that raised us on their own

And made the Government housing feel like a home.

The ones who worked 2 jobs to make sure that we ate.

The ones that endured and showed us love through the hate.,

She spanked, she yelled, she cooked.

She saw the good in people and read you like a book.

The ones who were there to pick you up if you fall.

The ones that picked up the phone whenever you called.

Whether you were in jail or the army.

Whether you were a junkie or a doctor.

I salute the strong African man and even the stronger African woman

Of our past, present, and future.

Walk Like A Lion

The rage of a man caged.

Should I be affected in a negative way?

Should I give freely the knowledge I've obtained?

Or should I defy the system to show my disdain?

I've never known a pain this intense.

Deep cuts, I keep from going nuts.

But wish I could jump the fence.

What does my face read?

I wonder if they can tell my heart bleeds.

I escape through my pen.

But deep down within

I'm still stuck with my sins.

So many days I've lost.

So many nights I've tossed.

What good is power?

When you realize that your power is false.

I face the music.

But I wonder how will I use it

I mean the music.

They say I have a way with words.

Sometimes in life we never get what we deserve.

Preparation at this moment

Is worth more than reparations.

The cash they give

Could never mask what I feel.

What good is a lions roar?

When the jungle is empty?

Nobody hears it. Nobody fears it.

So my desire is to be heard.

My expressions affect others

So I use them with wise discretion.

Hoping to one day paint the perfect picture.

And if it's the perfect picture

It must be a picture of perfection.

A hollow soul never earns respect.

So now you echo when you talk.

A soul that's whole has substance and character.

Just like the lion when he walks.

Joe Black

Man look you aint no crook.

You aint gotta snatch no pocketbooks.

Now you spending all the cash you took.

Had a mask on but the judge still threw the book.

At your trial your lawyer smiled.

You saw the jury crack a smile.

So, you decided to crack a smile.

All the while mama losing a child.

Now your sentenced for your crime.

Can't even calculate the time.

Aint leave your son and daughter a dime.

Now you lying when you say your fine.

And this the drama of Joe Black.

If it aint the guns then it's the crack

Once you come to prison you know you are black

It's easy to get here it's hard to get back.

And especially for Joe Black......

And especially for Joe Back.......

Face Value

For every action there is a consequence.

What you do in the dark will eventually come to the light.

My mama used to always tell me this.

And now I'm just realizing she was right.

Evil deeds and deceitful ways

Will catchup with you in due time.

You reap what you sow and I should know.

I'm mentally tortured by my life of crime.

It's not too late to leave the game.

Put down the guns and the crack cocaine.

To many brothers doing time in penitentiaries.

But we only have ourselves to blame.

We know we're risking our freedom and lives every day.

But yet we still hustle can't we find another way.

We think we know it all.

We give our all to the streets.

But do we ever take the time out to pray?

Young black America is looking more doomed every day.

I can laugh with you today.

But tomorrow my mother may have to bury me.

It's so sad for me to see all the senseless murder of my people.

The lack of respect in our communities.

We don't treat each other as equals.

Too much jealousy and hate.

Not enough love and encouragement.

It all about the so called, blood money.

Those dead presidents.

We must reevaluate our lives and get our priorities straight.

Cause problems aren't the only things that black men can create.

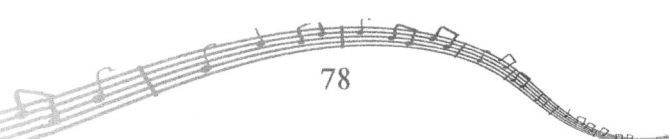

Wise Old Man

Where are you wise old man?

I need your guidance.

There are so many things that I don't understand.

I'm relying on you to give me knowledge

No man can take away.

A sense of direction so I'll know what path to take.

If you show interest in my life.

I may never spend time in jail.

You're so vital to my existence.

Without you I just may fail.

Teach me how to be a real man

Love my queen and raise my kids.

If you show me how to live as a righteous man

I promise to do everything you did.

I admire you from afar.

But how I wish you were much more close to me.

I want to mirror your image but it's hard.

I can sense that you are not concerned with me.

I was confused by so many situations

While becoming a man all alone.

Without you I took so many wrong turns

Mistakes I understand clearly now that I am grown.

If only you would have taken the time out

To school me with wisdom and good advice.

What a difference a wise old man could have made in a young mans life.

The Threat

I wonder when times get rough

Will we be courageous enough?

To stand steadfast with the strong

Or will the pressure make us self destruct?

Power to the people

Was once quoted by our ancestors with strong minds.

May my voice lead the people

Now that my heart has been refined.

Consider me the thorn in your side.

Why should I apologize?

When I fight for what's right

We are living dangerous black.

They consider us an inferior race.

But our mere presence

Turns the average setting

Into a superior place.

I can see light years away

African presidents on display.

There's no longer black history month.

We make black history every day.

We shall be acknowledged! You will accept our culture!

Yes this is a threat!

No matter what you do our value can not be diminshed.

The world will comply before we are finished!

Reflections Of An Inept Past (OL R.I.P.)

Oh there he go again, Ol R.I.P.

I call him R.I.P. because he's a dead man walking.

Now don't be alarmed when I tell you this.

The boy got a hell of a mouth piece.

He's also a dead man talking.

According to him a woman is a trick.

He can't stand a snitch.

And he don't give a damn about those crackers.

If da brother aint hustling riding on dubs

The nigga gots to be living backwards.

He says that he hates the white man

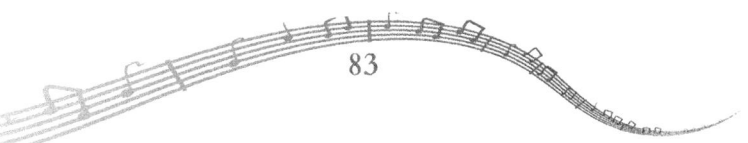

But they consider him a friend.

Y'all know why?

They're hoping he could disrupt the righteous black man.

Destroy him from within.

You know what I mean.

Get him off his square.

Follow me you aint no square.

You were there with the half naked women

Beer and weed in the air.

With the coke on the table

ready willing and able.

Dressed to a T in ya 1999 Lesabre.

You and ol R.I.P.

Or were you R.I.P.?

Or were you both R.I.P?

Two dummies with all the money.

Quick to hollar aint no game for free.

When are you going to get serious though?

When are you going to get some serious dough?

You can't even negotiate with the white folks.

You still got that curious flow.

I guess you stuck in the element.

Moving weight like an elephant.

Waiting on time like you a watch.

Don't worry you are going to catch the time.

Those that play the game always get a chance to watch.

Look at me I've been on the bench for ten years.

The judge said that I was a showboat

Who couldn't read DEFENSES very well.

So now I'm relegated to back up hustler.

My job description

Just what it says to back up the hustler.

So now when I see R.I.P.

I always make sure to leave him a piece of me.

Every chance I get I holler at the young cats

Give em a little bit of this and a little bit of that.

Trade war stories about the dope and the gats.

Tell em about Garvey and X mixed with a lil bit of 2pac
philosopy.

Don't want to lose them getting too deep.

The only language some of these kids speak is dialect from the
streets.

I just don't want them to grow up to be ol R.I.P.

Sometime I wonder why God left this up to me?

Oh well at least I aint in hell.

Or am I in hell?

Lord knows I've seen enough fire on my block

From the fiends and the glocks.

It's really hard to tell.

But I'll rather be in hell than to go back being ol R.I.P.

(REFLECTIONS OF AN INEPT PAST)

Today

Today I just don't feel like giving myself at all.

I want to be left alone.

The problems of the world are not mine.

How can I save people

Who don't want to be saved?

How can I free slaves

Who want to be slaves?

I have my own issues to deal with.

I feel as if my mother and grandmother are slowly dying.

And here I am writing a God damn book!

Trying to show the world a nigga in prison got a new outlook.

Today I feel like destroying this pen

And never again writing what I truly feel.

Can I really make a difference?

After ten years away

Who in the hell is going to listen?

I'm so frustrated with myself.

I'm frustrated with the mindset of men in this prison.

I'm frustrated with the world and this war with Iraq.

I'm frustrated with the media for constantly misrepresenting blacks.

Today I can honestly say fuck the world!

Ain't nobody help me in my time of need.

Ain't nobody try to prevent me from coming to prison.

Grown folks watched me fuck up and kept on living.

So why can't I live now?

Why God keep calling on me to heal?

I make no apologies for what I feel.

God blessed me with another day to live.

But my heart is just not in it today.

I pray I'll only feel this way.

The way I feel just today.

Proetry (Prison Poetry)

Through my time, I've outlasted many friends.

In my cell, I've had conversations with many dead men.

The murders, murders, murders, murders.!

Mothers across America are still distraught.

Haven't we learned anything

From what Malcolm and Martin taught?

Cocaine got us in the game.

Gave the no name nigga a name.

Got him some change and a fine ass dame

Helped him get a benz now he rolling on dem thangs.

What a deceptive depiction of living.

Is the hustler receptive to a divine vision?

A'int nothing wrong with bumping Pac.

But understand Tupac and realize why he was shot.

He lost control!

We lost control!

Get back into your true nature before you lose your soul.

The grim reaper digs deeper and deeper into my people.

I listen but the whole world stays silent.

Who really cares when it's black on black violence.

Whose Soul Is This?

Sometimes I feel as if I've been here before

Like this isn't my first life.

The more I'm in touch with my spirituality.

The more the creator seems to reveal to me.

I know answers to questions I've never studied.

I see visions of myself inspiring a nation.

Sometimes I don't want to believe

What I see and hear in my meditations.

But it's a feeling that I can't ignore

It's all real ever so real.

What am I being prepared for?

God whose soul is this?

There are days that I don't even feel mortal.

Why do I understand death so clearly?

Why do I ask questions to the unseen?

Why are the answers revealed so clearly?

I'm afraid of my new found powers.

I don't want to misuse or abuse them.

Theirs a stranger within my flesh.

Am I cursed or am I blessed?

Why me I ask?

Why have I been chosen for this task?

When I look in the mirror

I see my soul wearing a mask.

Whose underneath that mask?

This is not me that's somebody else spirit.

I'm confused and confined.

I need to know

Whose soul is this?

He Say She Say

Bush said that he said, that they said

That they got weapons of mass destruction.

And if they didn't clear my speech

We would have never went to Iraq busting.

But Bush you said, not they said or he said screw the U.N

when you launched the first missile attack

Without their support.

You said that you had a country to defend.

Now Colin Powell say

Not I say, or they say, or you say

That he is about to retire.

I guess Colin is black.

Yall see he got out of that fire.

Now they say, and you say, not I say or we say

That the war is officially over.

Now tell the truth Mr. Bush.

After the war was over we lost more soldiers.

Now you say, and they say, not we say or I say

That Saddam Hussein sons have been killed.

But somebody say they saw Saddam up north

in a Mcdonalds eating a happy meal.

Bush said, and they said not I said or we said

That he's going on a peace mission to Africa.

Yeah that sounds good Mr. President

But tell us really what you are after?

Donald Rumsfield said that Tony Blair said, that they said not
I said.

That he had reliable intelligence on this matter.

But the more yall talk it seems to the people

That this war started all over chit chatter.

Now I say and we say not Bush say or they say

That yall still aint found no weapons of mass destruction.

And yall wonder why the Iraqi people

cussin and fussin and they guns keep bustin.

Now I say and we say not yall say or Bush say

Yall need to watch all that he say, she say.

Because now a lot of people dead

And a lot of people scared.

All because of he say, she say.

Made in the USA
Monee, IL
16 July 2021